Biography Of Franklin Pierce

The Last Hope Before War: A President Caught Between Loyalty and Chaos

Graham Newberry

Table Of Contents

Introduction

The Forgotten President: A Legacy Reexamined

History is often unkind to those who find themselves trapped in the currents of division, and few American presidents embody this truth more than Franklin Pierce. Once a rising star of the Democratic Party, Pierce ascended to the presidency at a time when the nation teetered on the brink of catastrophe. His election in 1852 was hailed as a moment of unity, a chance to heal the wounds festering between North and South. Yet, by the time he left office, the country was more fractured than ever, and his legacy was stained by his inability—or unwillingness—to halt the march toward civil war.

Today, Franklin Pierce is largely forgotten, overshadowed by the titanic figures who came before and after him. Sandwiched between the transformative leadership of James K. Polk and the looming shadow of Abraham Lincoln, Pierce is often dismissed as a weak, indecisive leader who failed to rise to the occasion. His support for the Kansas-Nebraska Act, which reignited sectional tensions by allowing slavery to expand into new territories, is widely regarded as his defining—and most disastrous—political decision. Yet, to reduce his presidency to a single failure is to ignore the complexities of his time in office and the forces that shaped him.

Born in New Hampshire, Pierce was a man of contradictions: a Northerner who sympathized with the South, a leader who sought compromise but instead deepened national strife, and a politician whose personal charm could not mask his political missteps. His administration may have accelerated the nation's descent into war, but was Pierce truly the architect of that fate, or merely a casualty of a nation already hurtling toward destruction?

This book seeks to reexamine Franklin Pierce's presidency and legacy—not to absolve him of his faults, but to understand them. By exploring his rise to power, his time in the White House, and his post-presidential years, we will uncover the full story of a man who was both a product and a victim of his era. In doing so, we may find that the story of Franklin Pierce is not just a cautionary tale of failed leadership, but a mirror reflecting the deep divisions that continue to shape America today.

Chapter 1: Beginnings of a Leader

A New Hampshire Childhood

Franklin Pierce was born on November 23, 1804, in a small log cabin in Hillsborough, New Hampshire, a town nestled within the rugged, rural terrain of New England. His birth came at a time of great change in the young United States. The Revolutionary War had ended just two decades earlier, and the nation was still defining its identity, struggling to balance democracy with order. The people of New Hampshire were fiercely independent, shaped by the harsh winters and the necessity of self-reliance. This environment would leave an indelible mark on Pierce, shaping his character, values, and political outlook.

Pierce was the fifth of eight children born to Benjamin Pierce and Anna Kendrick Pierce. His father, a decorated Revolutionary War veteran, was a well-respected figure in the community, known for his leadership and military service. Benjamin Pierce had fought in some of the war's most critical battles, including Saratoga and Monmouth, and carried with him the pride of a self-made man who had risen through merit and determination. His achievements earned him the role of a local militia leader and, later, a two-term governor of New Hampshire.

Despite the respect his father commanded, the Pierce family was far from wealthy. They lived modestly, relying on farming to sustain themselves. Franklin Pierce's childhood was one of labor and discipline, as he and his siblings were expected to contribute to the household. The demands of farm life instilled in him a strong work ethic but also exposed him to the struggles of working-class Americans, a perspective that later shaped his political sympathies.

The political culture of Hillsborough was lively, with town meetings serving as a forum for heated debates about state and national affairs. From an early age, Franklin was exposed to discussions about governance, democracy, and the role of leadership. He would often listen to his father speak about the responsibilities of public service and the sacrifices required of those in power. These conversations planted the seeds of ambition in young Franklin, though his early years did not immediately suggest he was destined for greatness.

The Influence of a Political Father

Benjamin Pierce was not just a father to Franklin; he was a model of leadership, resilience, and public service. A staunch Jeffersonian Democrat, he believed in the virtues of the common man and distrusted aristocratic elites. His political ideology emphasized individual freedoms, a limited federal government, and the expansion of opportunity to those outside the traditional power structures.

As governor of New Hampshire, Benjamin Pierce wielded considerable influence in state politics. He upheld the values of the Democratic-Republican Party, championing policies that benefited farmers, small business owners, and laborers. His commitment to the people of

New Hampshire earned him both admiration and enemies, but he remained unwavering in his convictions.

Franklin grew up in an environment where politics was not just a profession but a duty. He saw firsthand the power his father wielded—not in personal gain, but in shaping the lives of others. Watching his father govern with integrity and purpose instilled in Franklin a deep respect for public service. However, he also witnessed the toll that politics could take. Benjamin Pierce's career was marked by both triumphs and personal sacrifices, teaching Franklin that leadership often came with great burdens.

Despite this strong influence, Franklin Pierce was not an exceptional student in his early years. Unlike his father, who had risen through the ranks of the military through sheer grit, Franklin struggled with academics and was often more interested in socializing than studying. His father, however, refused to let him succumb to mediocrity. Believing in his son's potential, Benjamin Pierce ensured that Franklin received a formal education, sending him to Hancock Academy and later to Phillips Exeter Academy, one of New England's most prestigious preparatory schools.

It was here that Franklin's trajectory began to change. Although he initially lagged behind his peers, he eventually developed a newfound discipline and determination to succeed. This transformation was due in part to his father's encouragement, but also to his own realization that education was the gateway to leadership. By the time he was ready to enter college, Franklin Pierce had shed the image of an unremarkable student and had begun to embrace his potential.

Education, Ambition, and Early Law Career

At the age of 15, Franklin Pierce enrolled at Bowdoin College in Brunswick, Maine, a decision that would further shape his path. Bowdoin was a small but respected institution, known for producing future leaders in politics, literature, and the law. Among his classmates were Nathaniel Hawthorne, who would go on to become one of America's most celebrated novelists, and Henry Wadsworth Longfellow, the famed poet. These friendships would endure throughout his life, particularly his bond with Hawthorne, who later wrote Pierce's campaign biography during his run for the presidency.

Pierce's time at Bowdoin was transformative. Though he continued to enjoy socializing, he also began to demonstrate intellectual curiosity and leadership potential. He was deeply interested in history, philosophy, and the workings of government. More importantly, he discovered a talent for rhetoric and debate, skills that would serve him well in his future career. By the time he graduated in 1824, he had cultivated both the discipline and the ambition necessary for a career in law and politics.

Following his graduation, Pierce studied law under the mentorship of Levi Woodbury, a prominent Democratic politician who would later serve as a U.S. senator and Supreme Court justice. Woodbury was a powerful figure in New Hampshire politics and an early supporter of Andrew Jackson, whose populist ideals would later influence Pierce's own political philosophy. Under Woodbury's guidance, Pierce developed a keen understanding of the legal system and the role it played in shaping society.

After completing his legal studies, Pierce was admitted to the New Hampshire bar in 1827. He quickly established a law practice in Concord, the state capital, where he gained a reputation for his eloquence and sharp legal mind. His ability to connect with juries, particularly working-class citizens, made him a successful attorney. Unlike some of his contemporaries who approached law as an intellectual pursuit, Pierce saw it as a tool for advocating for ordinary people. His legal work often put him in close contact with farmers, laborers, and small business owners, further shaping his Democratic leanings.

But the law was never Pierce's final ambition—politics was. He understood that the path to leadership lay not just in legal expertise, but in public service. In 1829, at just 24 years old, he was elected to the New Hampshire state legislature. It was a rapid ascent, reflecting both his father's influence and his own growing reputation. In the legislature, he quickly made a name for himself as a skilled orator and a rising force within the Democratic Party.

Pierce's early political career coincided with the rise of Andrew Jackson, whose populist, anti-elitist message resonated deeply with him. Like Jackson, Pierce saw himself as a champion of the common man, someone who could bridge the divide between the government and the people. His political instincts, combined with his charm and eloquence, made him a natural leader within the party. By 1833, he had been elected to the U.S. House of Representatives, marking the beginning of his national political career.

Franklin Pierce's journey from a small-town boy in New Hampshire to a rising political figure was shaped by many factors—his father's influence, his education, and his early success in law and politics. But at the heart of his story was an unwavering belief in leadership as a duty. While his early years hinted at the ambition that would define his career, they also foreshadowed the struggles he would later face: the challenge of balancing ideals with political realities, and the difficulty of leading a divided nation.

As Pierce moved from the New Hampshire legislature to Washington, his path seemed destined for greater heights. But with opportunity came obstacles, and the choices he made in the years to come would determine not just his fate, but the fate of a nation teetering on the edge of conflict.

Chapter 2: The Rise in Politics

A Young Legislator in Washington

Franklin Pierce's rise in national politics was both swift and strategic. Elected to the U.S. House of Representatives in 1833 at just 28 years old, he became one of the youngest members of Congress. His early political career was marked by enthusiasm, loyalty to the Democratic Party, and a keen ability to build relationships with key political figures. Despite his youth, Pierce quickly positioned himself as a promising leader, earning the respect of his colleagues through his eloquence, sharp political instincts, and unwavering commitment to his party's principles.

Washington, D.C., in the early 1830s was a turbulent and deeply divided political landscape. The nation was grappling with the rise of sectional tensions, economic instability, and fierce debates over federal power. As a Democratic representative from New Hampshire, Pierce aligned himself with the party's populist ideals, advocating for policies that supported small farmers, working-class citizens, and states' rights. His early legislative work focused on issues important to his home state, such as economic development, infrastructure improvements, and expanding political opportunities for ordinary Americans.

Unlike many young legislators who struggled to make their mark, Pierce distinguished himself through his ability to connect with people. He was not a policy wonk or a revolutionary thinker; rather, he excelled at reading political currents, understanding the needs of his constituents, and using his charm and persuasive abilities to influence debates. His speeches, though not always groundbreaking, were powerful in their delivery and resonated with fellow lawmakers who admired his sincerity and conviction.

One of the defining moments of his early legislative career was his opposition to the abolitionist movement. Like many Northern Democrats of his time, Pierce believed that slavery was a divisive issue that should be left to the states. Though personally uncomfortable with the institution, he feared that aggressive abolitionist policies would disrupt the fragile unity between North and South. This stance earned him both support and criticism, as he walked the fine line between appeasing Southern Democrats and maintaining his credibility in the North.

By 1837, Pierce's growing influence and strong ties within the Democratic Party led to his election to the U.S. Senate—the youngest senator in the nation at the time. His tenure in the Senate solidified his reputation as a dedicated party loyalist and a skilled negotiator. He worked closely with Democratic leaders on key legislation, supported President Martin Van Buren's economic policies, and played a role in the ongoing debates over tariffs, banking regulations, and state sovereignty.

However, despite his rising profile, Pierce's time in Washington was not without challenges. He struggled with the demands of national politics, particularly the growing sectional tensions that threatened to tear the country apart. His commitment to party unity often forced him to take positions that were politically expedient rather than morally driven. This pragmatic approach, while effective in securing his political advancement, foreshadowed the struggles he would face as a national leader in the years to come.

The Jacksonian Influence

Perhaps the most significant influence on Pierce's political ideology was President Andrew Jackson, the fiery and controversial leader who reshaped American politics in the 1830s. Jackson's presidency was defined by his fierce populism, distrust of centralized power, and deep loyalty to the Democratic Party. His leadership style and policies left an indelible mark on Pierce, shaping his views on governance, democracy, and national unity.

Jackson's belief in the "common man" resonated deeply with Pierce, who had grown up in a working-class environment in New Hampshire. Like Jackson, Pierce believed that political power should rest with the people, rather than with elites in Washington. He embraced the Democratic Party's opposition to aristocratic privilege and saw himself as a defender of farmers, laborers, and small business owners.

One of the most controversial aspects of Jackson's presidency was his war against the Second Bank of the United States. Jackson viewed the national bank as a corrupt institution that favored wealthy elites over ordinary Americans. Pierce, like many other Jacksonian Democrats, supported the dismantling of the bank, arguing that it concentrated too much power in the hands of a few. This position further cemented his reputation as a champion of states' rights and economic populism.

Another key issue that defined the Jacksonian era—and Pierce's own political philosophy—was the growing debate over federal versus state authority. Jackson's forceful handling of the Nullification Crisis in 1832, in which South Carolina attempted to reject federal tariffs, demonstrated his belief in preserving the Union at all costs. While Pierce admired Jackson's commitment to national unity, he was also wary of using federal power too aggressively. This tension between upholding the Union and respecting states' rights would later become a defining challenge of his presidency.

Beyond policy, Jackson's leadership style also left a lasting impression on Pierce. Jackson was a firm believer in party loyalty and the spoils system, which rewarded political supporters with government positions. Pierce adopted a similar approach, surrounding himself with trusted allies and prioritizing party unity above ideological purity. This loyalty to the Democratic establishment helped him rise through the ranks but also made him resistant to political compromise—an attitude that would later contribute to his struggles as president.

Personal Tragedy and Political Growth

While Pierce's political career flourished during the late 1830s and early 1840s, his personal life was marked by profound tragedy. In 1834, he married Jane Means Appleton, the daughter of a prominent New England family. Unlike her husband, Jane was deeply religious, introverted, and intensely private. She despised politics and viewed Washington as a corrupt and dangerous place. Despite their differences, the couple shared a deep bond, though Jane's fragile health and aversion to public life created tensions throughout their marriage.

The couple suffered a series of devastating personal losses that would haunt Pierce for the rest of his life. Of their three children, none survived into adulthood. Their first child, Franklin Jr., passed away as an infant. Their second child, Frank Robert, succumbed to typhus at just four years old. But the most traumatic loss came in 1853 when their third son, Benjamin, was killed in a train accident at the age of 11—just weeks before Pierce's presidential inauguration.

These tragedies had a profound impact on Pierce's psyche and outlook. While he remained dedicated to his political ambitions, the weight of personal grief often overshadowed his successes. His wife, Jane, became increasingly withdrawn, blaming politics for their misfortunes and viewing her husband's career as a curse. Her deep sorrow and disapproval of public life created a constant emotional burden for Pierce, who struggled to reconcile his professional aspirations with his family's suffering.

Despite these hardships, Pierce's political career continued to advance. In 1842, he made the surprising decision to resign from the Senate, citing a desire to return to private life and care for his family. However, his withdrawal from Washington was short-lived. He remained deeply involved in New Hampshire politics, serving as a prominent Democratic leader and adviser. His legal practice thrived, and he became known as one of the most skilled attorneys in the state.

Pierce's temporary retreat from national politics did not diminish his influence. In fact, it strengthened his position as a party loyalist who could be called upon when needed. His unwavering commitment to the Democratic cause, combined with his personal charisma and legal expertise, made him a natural choice for future leadership roles.

As the 1840s progressed, the United States found itself increasingly embroiled in debates over territorial expansion and the spread of slavery. The Mexican-American War (1846–1848) presented an opportunity for Pierce to re-enter national politics in a new capacity. His service in the war, though brief, boosted his public image and solidified his reputation as a patriotic leader willing to make personal sacrifices for his country.

By the end of the decade, Pierce was no longer just a rising political star—he was a seasoned leader with the experience, connections, and party loyalty necessary to ascend to the highest office in the land. However, the very qualities that had propelled him forward—his devotion to party unity, his resistance to ideological conflict, and his belief in compromise—would soon be tested in ways he had never imagined.

As Franklin Pierce's political journey continued, he would find himself at the center of one of the most contentious periods in American history. His rise to power was shaped by ambition, loyalty, and personal resilience, but his ultimate legacy would be determined by how he navigated the storm of national crisis that lay ahead.

Chapter 3: War and Honor

Volunteering for the Mexican-American War

By the mid-1840s, Franklin Pierce had already established himself as a respected political leader in New Hampshire and a devoted Democratic Party loyalist. However, his decision to volunteer for military service during the Mexican-American War (1846–1848) marked a turning point in his career, transforming him from a regional politician into a national figure.

The war, initiated by President James K. Polk, was deeply controversial. While many Americans supported the idea of territorial expansion, others, particularly abolitionists, feared that the conflict was an excuse to expand slavery into newly acquired lands. Pierce, a staunch Democrat and an ardent supporter of the war, saw it as a patriotic duty and an opportunity to serve his country beyond the political arena. His decision to enlist was not merely symbolic—he sought an active role in combat, eager to prove his leadership and dedication to the Union.

Pierce's motivations were a combination of personal ambition and genuine nationalism. By volunteering, he reinforced his loyalty to the Democratic Party, which was largely in favor of expansionism, while also positioning himself for future political opportunities. Unlike some politicians who saw military service as a way to boost their public image without real sacrifice, Pierce sought an actual command position, where he could directly contribute to the war effort.

His appointment as a brigadier general in 1847 came despite his lack of prior military experience. However, his legal and political background had made him well-versed in matters of governance and organization, which were crucial for military leadership. Additionally, his charisma and ability to inspire loyalty among troops made him a natural choice for command.

Leadership on the Battlefield

Pierce was assigned to serve under General Winfield Scott, one of the most accomplished military leaders of the time. Scott was leading a major campaign in central Mexico, aiming to capture Mexico City and force the Mexican government into surrender. Pierce's role was to command a brigade within the army's advancing force.

Despite his enthusiasm, Pierce's military experience was marked by both determination and hardship. He was tasked with leading troops through difficult terrain, managing supply lines, and engaging in skirmishes with Mexican forces. His leadership was put to the test in several battles, including the pivotal Battle of Contreras in August 1847.

It was during this battle that Pierce's resolve was truly challenged. As his brigade advanced through rugged, rain-soaked terrain, he suffered a severe injury after falling from his horse. His knee was badly wounded, leaving him in intense pain and struggling to continue leading his men. For many soldiers, such an injury would have meant immediate withdrawal from the battlefield. However, Pierce refused to be removed from combat.

Determined to fulfill his duty, he had himself strapped to his saddle and continued forward with his troops. This act of resilience earned him the admiration of his men, reinforcing his reputation as a leader who would not abandon his post, no matter the circumstances. Though physically weakened, he pushed through the remainder of the campaign, enduring both the harsh realities of war and the personal discomfort of his injury.

However, his injury ultimately proved debilitating. By the time of the final assault on Mexico City, Pierce was unable to play a direct role in combat. His inability to participate in the final victory frustrated him deeply, as he had hoped to be at the forefront of the war's most decisive moment. Despite this, his earlier leadership contributions did not go unnoticed, and his name was added to the list of commanders who had played a key role in the campaign.

The Mexican-American War was a brutal conflict, and its legacy remains contested. For Pierce, it was both a defining experience and a source of lasting pride. Though his battlefield leadership was not as celebrated as that of generals like Scott or Zachary Taylor, his resilience and unwavering dedication to his troops left a strong impression on those who served under him.

Returning as a War Hero

By the time the war ended in 1848, Franklin Pierce had solidified his status as a national figure. Though he had not led troops in any decisive victories, his commitment to the war effort and his personal sacrifices made him a respected veteran. More importantly, his return home as a war hero gave him newfound political credibility, setting the stage for his eventual rise to the presidency.

The Democratic Party, still the dominant force in national politics, was eager to elevate leaders who had proven their loyalty and service to the country. The war had made military figures incredibly popular, with generals like Zachary Taylor and Winfield Scott emerging as presidential contenders. While Pierce was not at their level in terms of battlefield accomplishments, his service provided him with a crucial political advantage: he could present himself as both a statesman and a patriot who had put his country above personal gain.

Upon returning to New Hampshire, Pierce was greeted with widespread admiration. His war record helped him reconnect with voters and strengthen his standing within the Democratic Party. He resumed his legal practice but remained deeply involved in state and national politics. His experience in the war had also reinforced his belief in national unity and the importance of preserving the balance between North and South—an issue that would dominate his later presidency.

However, his return was also marked by personal challenges. His wife, Jane, had always opposed his involvement in politics and was horrified by his decision to serve in the war. She viewed his military service as reckless and unnecessary, blaming it for his injury and fearing it would draw him further into public life. Their relationship, already strained by previous tragedies, became even more fragile. Despite Jane's objections, Pierce could not ignore the momentum his military service had given him.

As the 1850s began, the nation was inching closer to a full-blown sectional crisis. Debates over slavery, territorial expansion, and federal authority were intensifying, and the Democratic Party was searching for a leader who could navigate these turbulent waters. Pierce's war service, combined with his reputation as a loyal Democrat and a unifier, made him an increasingly appealing candidate for national office.

While Franklin Pierce had entered the Mexican-American War as a relatively unknown political figure outside New England, he emerged from it as a national leader with a compelling narrative of service and sacrifice. His time on the battlefield, though physically taxing and at times frustrating, had transformed him into a viable presidential contender.

The war had given him honor, but it had also given him responsibility. The next chapter of his life would test whether he could translate his battlefield resilience into effective leadership at the highest level of American politics.

Chapter 4: The Road to the Presidency

The 1852 Democratic Convention Surprise

Franklin Pierce's ascent to the presidency was anything but predictable. By the early 1850s, he was a respected political figure in New Hampshire but was not considered a national heavyweight within the Democratic Party. In fact, he had been absent from major political office for nearly a decade, focusing on his legal career and family life after resigning from the Senate in 1842. However, the Democratic Party of 1852 was deeply fractured, and Pierce's reputation as a loyal, uncontroversial party man ultimately played in his favor.

The lead-up to the 1852 Democratic National Convention was characterized by fierce competition among several prominent candidates. Senator Lewis Cass, who had lost the presidency to Zachary Taylor in 1848, was attempting another bid. Former Secretary of State James Buchanan and Senator Stephen A. Douglas were also leading contenders. Each of these men had substantial political experience and dedicated factions of supporters, but they were also divisive figures within the party.

The convention, held in Baltimore in June 1852, quickly descended into deadlock. Despite dozens of ballots, none of the leading candidates could secure the necessary two-thirds majority required for nomination. This stalemate created an opening for a dark horse candidate—someone who could unite the warring factions of the party.

Pierce's name was initially mentioned as a compromise candidate by his New Hampshire allies, but few took his chances seriously. However, behind the scenes, influential Democratic leaders were searching for an alternative—someone with strong party loyalty, a record of service, and, most importantly, no major enemies. Pierce fit this description perfectly.

His relative obscurity became his greatest strength. Unlike Cass, Buchanan, or Douglas, he had not been involved in the most contentious debates of the era, particularly those regarding slavery expansion and sectional tensions. His military service in the Mexican-American War further bolstered his appeal, allowing Democrats to frame him as a patriotic leader despite his lack of executive experience.

After 48 ballots, Pierce's momentum surged, and on the 49th ballot, he secured the Democratic nomination. The surprise victory shocked the political establishment. Pierce had not actively campaigned for the nomination, and his sudden emergence as the Democratic standard-bearer was a testament to both the party's internal divisions and his own reputation as a unifying figure.

Campaigning for Unity in a Divided Nation

With the nomination secured, Pierce and his party faced a formidable challenge: winning the presidency in a nation that was growing increasingly divided over the issue of slavery. The Compromise of 1850 had temporarily eased tensions between the North and South, but the underlying conflicts remained unresolved. Many Americans feared that the country was heading toward a larger crisis, and the presidential election of 1852 would serve as a critical moment in determining the nation's future direction.

The Whig Party, which had won the previous two presidential elections, nominated General Winfield Scott, Pierce's former commander in the

Mexican-American War. Scott was a celebrated military leader but lacked strong political instincts. Additionally, the Whigs were deeply fractured, particularly over the issue of slavery. Southern Whigs distrusted Scott, believing he was too sympathetic to Northern anti-slavery interests, while Northern Whigs viewed him as too accommodating to the South. This internal division would prove disastrous for the Whig campaign.

Pierce, in contrast, ran a campaign focused on national unity and party loyalty. His platform emphasized the importance of upholding the Compromise of 1850, which included the controversial Fugitive Slave Act. While personally opposed to slavery, Pierce was a staunch believer in maintaining the Union and adhering to the Constitution, which meant supporting laws that protected Southern interests. His message reassured Southern Democrats that he would not pursue anti-slavery policies, while also appealing to moderate Northern voters who wanted to avoid further sectional conflict.

The Democratic campaign was highly organized, with party operatives working tirelessly to portray Pierce as a patriotic leader and devoted statesman. His military service was frequently highlighted, and his personal background—a man of humble origins who had risen through hard work and dedication—resonated with many voters. The campaign also benefitted from the growing weakness of the Whig Party, which struggled to present a coherent message to the electorate.

Another key factor in Pierce's favor was his running mate, William R. King of Alabama.

King was a veteran politician and a strong advocate for Southern interests, which helped balance the ticket and reassure pro-slavery Democrats that Pierce would not betray them. Though King was ill during much of the campaign (and would die shortly after being inaugurated as vice president), his presence on the ticket played a crucial role in securing Southern support.

Despite his strong showing in the campaign, Pierce personally did little public speaking. Following the tradition of the time, he did not actively campaign, leaving most of the work to party leaders and newspapers. Instead, he maintained a dignified distance, allowing his supporters to shape his image and promote his candidacy.

The Landslide Victory and National Expectations

When the election results came in, they revealed a resounding victory for Franklin Pierce. He won 27 of the 31 states, securing 254 electoral votes to Scott's 42. The popular vote margin was also decisive, with Pierce receiving approximately 51% compared to Scott's 44%. This overwhelming victory signaled the complete collapse of the Whig Party as a national force, as divisions within their ranks had crippled their ability to compete effectively.

Pierce's triumph was, in part, a reflection of Democratic dominance rather than personal popularity. The Whigs struggled to unite behind a common platform, while the Democrats, despite their own internal differences, had presented a more cohesive message. The election also highlighted the growing sectional tensions within the country—while Pierce had broad support across most states, the underlying conflicts over slavery and national identity remained unresolved.

As he prepared to assume the presidency, expectations were high. His supporters believed that his emphasis on unity and compromise would help stabilize the nation and prevent further sectional discord. Many viewed his overwhelming victory as a mandate to uphold the Compromise of 1850 and maintain the fragile peace between North and South.

However, challenges loomed on the horizon. The country was not truly united, despite the election results, and the issues of slavery and territorial expansion continued to dominate political discourse. Pierce himself would soon face difficult decisions that would test his ability to govern effectively.

Moreover, his personal life was marked by deep tragedy in the wake of his election. Just weeks before his inauguration, his son, Benjamin, was killed in a horrific train accident. The loss devastated both Pierce and his wife, Jane, casting a shadow over his presidency even before it began. Jane, who had always been opposed to her husband's political ambitions, became withdrawn, and Pierce himself struggled with grief. This personal hardship would affect his leadership and decision-making during his time in office.

Despite these challenges, Franklin Pierce entered the presidency with immense political capital. He had won a landslide election, commanded the full support of his party, and was positioned to implement his vision of national unity. However, the very forces that had propelled him to victory—the Democratic Party's commitment to compromise and the fragile peace of the Compromise of 1850—would soon unravel, plunging the nation into deeper turmoil.

As the youngest president elected at the time, Pierce had the opportunity to reshape the political landscape. Yet, the road ahead was fraught with obstacles, and his ability to navigate them would determine his legacy. The coming years would test whether the man who had risen so unexpectedly to power could truly meet the expectations placed upon him.

Chapter 5: A Fragile Union Under Pressure

The Challenges of a Deeply Divided Country

By the time Franklin Pierce assumed the presidency in March 1853, the United States was a nation teetering on the brink of crisis. Although the Compromise of 1850 had temporarily eased tensions between the North and South, it had failed to address the underlying conflicts regarding slavery's expansion into new territories. Instead, the compromise had only delayed the inevitable showdown between free and slave states, and Pierce was now tasked with leading a country where sectional divisions were growing deeper with each passing year.

Pierce, a staunch Democrat and advocate of states' rights, believed that adherence to the Constitution and the rule of law would be enough to maintain national unity. He had campaigned on a platform of strict enforcement of the Compromise of 1850, including the controversial Fugitive Slave Act, which required free states to return escaped enslaved individuals to the South. While this policy reassured Southerners, it outraged many Northerners, who saw it as a moral betrayal and an infringement on their states' sovereignty.

Despite his intentions to preserve harmony, Pierce's presidency began amid an increasingly polarized political climate. The two-party system was fracturing, with the Whig Party collapsing under the weight of its divisions. Meanwhile, new political factions, including the emerging

Republican Party, were gaining traction by positioning themselves against the expansion of slavery.

Economic challenges also added to the nation's instability. Rapid industrialization in the North was creating a distinct economic system that clashed with the agrarian, slave-dependent economy of the South. These economic differences fueled political disputes, as Southern leaders feared the growing power of Northern industry and anti-slavery sentiment.

As Pierce sought to navigate this volatile landscape, he found himself caught between competing pressures. On one side, pro-slavery advocates demanded that the federal government protect their institution and allow slavery to expand westward. On the other, abolitionists and Northern free-soil supporters insisted that slavery should not spread any further. Pierce's attempts to please both sides ultimately satisfied neither, setting the stage for one of the most consequential decisions of his presidency—the Kansas-Nebraska Act.

The Kansas-Nebraska Act: A Fatal Decision

Of all the policies enacted during Pierce's presidency, none would prove more disastrous than the Kansas-Nebraska Act of 1854. Initially intended to promote westward expansion and economic development, the act instead reignited the slavery debate and pushed the nation closer to civil war.

The legislation, proposed by Illinois Senator Stephen A. Douglas, sought to organize the vast western territories acquired through the Louisiana Purchase. Douglas, a strong believer in popular sovereignty, argued that the settlers of each new territory should have the right to decide for themselves whether to allow slavery. This principle was at the heart of the Kansas-Nebraska Act, which effectively repealed the Missouri Compromise of 1820.

The Missouri Compromise had long served as a fragile peacekeeping measure, prohibiting slavery in all territories north of the 36°30' latitude, except for Missouri. By overturning this agreement, the Kansas-Nebraska Act opened the door for slavery to expand into regions that had been free for over three decades.

Pierce, eager to support his party's Southern wing and maintain Democratic unity, threw his full weight behind the bill. He saw it as a way to resolve the slavery question through democratic means, allowing local settlers to make their own decisions rather than having Congress impose a solution. However, he failed to recognize the explosive consequences of such a policy.

The act's passage in May 1854 unleashed immediate chaos. Northerners viewed it as a blatant surrender to the pro-slavery faction, while Southerners saw it as a victory for their interests. Almost overnight, the political landscape shifted. The Whig Party, already in decline, collapsed entirely as anti-slavery Whigs defected to new movements like the Free Soil Party and the emerging Republican Party.

But the most direct and violent consequences of the act occurred in the territories themselves. Kansas, in particular, became a battleground for the nation's deepening divisions. Pro-slavery and anti-slavery settlers flooded into the region, hoping to sway the vote in their favor. This led to the outbreak of what became known as "Bleeding Kansas"—a series of violent clashes between rival factions.

Armed militias from Missouri, known as "Border Ruffians," crossed into Kansas to illegally vote for pro-slavery candidates, while abolitionists from the North sent weapons and settlers to counteract them. The situation spiraled into bloodshed, with massacres and retaliatory attacks occurring throughout the territory.

Pierce's response to the violence was widely criticized. Instead of condemning the pro-slavery forces that had instigated much of the conflict, his administration largely sided with them, recognizing the fraudulent pro-slavery government in Kansas while dismissing the legitimacy of the anti-slavery faction. This stance alienated Northern Democrats and further divided the country.

The Kansas-Nebraska Act, rather than resolving the slavery debate, had made it even more inescapable. By attempting to appease both sides, Pierce had instead inflamed tensions beyond control, leaving his presidency permanently stained by the failure to maintain peace.

The Rise of Sectional Tensions

In the wake of the Kansas-Nebraska Act, sectional divisions in the United States became more pronounced than ever before. The issue of slavery, once managed through uneasy compromises, now dominated national politics in a way that made further reconciliation nearly impossible.

The immediate political impact of the act was the rapid rise of the Republican Party. Founded in 1854, the party was built around the central goal of preventing slavery from expanding into new territories. While its membership included former Whigs, Free Soilers, and Northern Democrats, its defining characteristic was its staunch opposition to the pro-slavery policies of the Pierce administration.

The Democratic Party, meanwhile, was also fracturing along sectional lines. Many Northern Democrats, appalled by Pierce's handling of the Kansas crisis, began distancing themselves from their Southern counterparts. While the party remained dominant at the national level for the time being, the internal divisions were becoming harder to ignore.

Social tensions also escalated as the national debate over slavery intensified. The publication of Harriet Beecher Stowe's Uncle Tom's Cabin in 1852 had already stirred anti-slavery sentiment across the North, portraying the brutal realities of slavery in a way that deeply resonated with readers. As violence in Kansas escalated, more Northerners began viewing the institution of slavery not as a political issue, but as a profound moral wrong that had to be opposed at all costs.

The South, in response, became more defensive and militant in its stance. Pro-slavery politicians, feeling increasingly threatened by the North's growing opposition, doubled down on their demands for federal protection of slavery. The idea of secession, once considered extreme, began gaining traction among Southern leaders who feared that the institution upon which their economy depended was under existential threat.

Pierce, rather than acting as a unifier, found himself overwhelmed by these growing tensions. His presidency, which had begun with high hopes for maintaining national stability, was now marked by escalating violence and political disintegration. His unwavering support for the South and his failure to address the crisis in Kansas effectively destroyed his chances for re-election.

By the time his term ended in 1857, the damage had been done. The Democratic Party had lost significant ground in the North, and the Republicans were emerging as a formidable opposition force. The country was more divided than ever, with the specter of civil war looming on the horizon.

In the end, Franklin Pierce's presidency exemplified the perils of attempting to govern through compromise when the fundamental question of slavery made true consensus impossible. His decisions, particularly his backing of the Kansas-Nebraska Act, did not preserve the Union but instead pushed it further toward its eventual rupture. The fragile balance that had held the nation together for decades was unraveling, and within just a few years, the United States would descend into the bloodiest conflict in its history.

Chapter 6: Foreign Policy and Expansion

Franklin Pierce's presidency was defined by domestic turmoil, particularly the sectional divisions over slavery. However, his administration also pursued an ambitious foreign policy agenda, reflecting the Democratic Party's expansionist goals and belief in Manifest Destiny. While Pierce sought to strengthen U.S. influence abroad, his administration's efforts—most notably the Ostend Manifesto—often sparked controversy. His foreign policy initiatives, though sometimes overshadowed by domestic crises, played a key role in shaping America's relationship with the world and its expansionist ambitions.

The Ostend Manifesto and Cuba Controversy

One of the most notorious foreign policy episodes of Pierce's presidency was the Ostend Manifesto, a secret diplomatic effort aimed at acquiring Cuba from Spain. This initiative was driven by a combination of economic, strategic, and ideological motivations.

By the mid-19th century, Cuba was a highly desirable territory for the United States. The island's economy, centered around sugar plantations, was deeply tied to the system of slavery, making it particularly appealing to Southern expansionists. Many Southerners viewed Cuba as a natural extension of the slaveholding South, a way to strengthen their political power as the North continued to grow in population and influence. Additionally, Cuba's proximity to Florida made it a valuable strategic asset for controlling shipping routes in the Caribbean.

Pierce, a supporter of Manifest Destiny, sought to acquire Cuba diplomatically. In 1854, he authorized three U.S. ministers—Pierre Soulé (minister to Spain), James Buchanan (minister to Britain), and John Mason (minister to France)—to meet in Ostend, Belgium, and develop a strategy for negotiating Cuba's purchase. The resulting document, known as the Ostend Manifesto, stated that the United States should attempt to buy Cuba from Spain for $120 million. However, the manifesto also suggested that if Spain refused, the U.S. would be justified in taking the island by force, citing national security concerns.

When news of the manifesto leaked, it caused an uproar. Northern politicians and abolitionists condemned it as a blatant attempt to expand slavery, while European powers viewed it as an aggressive act of American imperialism. The Pierce administration, already weakened by domestic instability, was forced to distance itself from the document, and the plan to acquire Cuba was abandoned.

The Ostend Manifesto ultimately backfired, further inflaming sectional tensions at home. It reinforced the growing perception that the Democratic Party was controlled by pro-slavery interests and weakened Pierce's credibility. While the idea of annexing Cuba remained a long-term goal for many American expansionists, the controversy surrounding the manifesto ensured that it would not be pursued under Pierce's leadership.

Strengthening U.S. Influence Abroad

Despite the failure of the Ostend Manifesto, the Pierce administration did make significant strides in expanding U.S. influence on the global stage. One of its most notable achievements was the negotiation of the Gadsden Purchase, which secured land in present-day southern Arizona and New Mexico.

The Gadsden Purchase was driven by the desire to build a southern transcontinental railroad that would connect the eastern United States to California. James Gadsden, the U.S. minister to Mexico, was tasked with negotiating the acquisition of land that would provide a suitable route for the railroad. In 1854, the U.S. and Mexico reached an agreement, with the U.S.

purchasing 29,670 square miles of territory for $10 million.

The acquisition of this land was significant for several reasons. First, it ensured a viable path for a southern railroad, which would facilitate commerce and migration to the West. Second, it helped improve U.S.-Mexico relations following the tensions of the Mexican-American War. While some critics viewed the purchase as an unnecessary expenditure, it ultimately contributed to America's broader expansionist goals.

Beyond North America, the Pierce administration sought to enhance U.S. trade and diplomatic relations in the Pacific. The United States had long been interested in expanding its commercial presence in Asia, and Pierce continued the efforts that had begun under previous administrations.

One of the most important developments in this regard was the Treaty of Kanagawa, negotiated by Commodore Matthew Perry in 1854. While the treaty had been initiated under President Millard Fillmore, its implementation fell under Pierce's administration. The agreement opened Japan to American trade, ending centuries of isolationist policies and establishing a foundation for future diplomatic and economic exchanges.

Pierce also looked to strengthen ties with Central and South America, recognizing the importance of maintaining stability in the region to protect U.S. commercial interests. His administration engaged in negotiations to expand trade with nations like Brazil and sought to assert U.S. influence over

European colonial ambitions in the Western Hemisphere. While these efforts were not always successful, they reflected America's growing global ambitions.

Navigating International Challenges

While Pierce aimed to expand American influence abroad, his administration also had to navigate a series of diplomatic challenges. International relations were complex in the mid-19th century, with European powers still holding strong colonial interests in the Americas and tensions simmering in various regions.

One of the key issues that Pierce faced was the increasing British presence in Central America. Britain had long maintained economic and strategic interests in the region, particularly in what is now Belize (then British Honduras) and the Mosquito Coast of present-day Nicaragua. The United States, following the Monroe Doctrine, viewed European intervention in the Western Hemisphere as a potential threat.

The Clayton-Bulwer Treaty of 1850, signed between the U.S. and Britain, had sought to prevent either nation from unilaterally controlling any canal that might be built through Central America. However, disputes over its interpretation led to rising tensions during Pierce's presidency. While Pierce did not take aggressive action against Britain, his administration sought to assert American dominance in the region, laying the groundwork for future confrontations over Central American influence.

Another significant challenge was the growing instability in Latin America. Revolutions and civil wars in countries like Mexico and Nicaragua threatened to disrupt American trade and investment.

Some American adventurers, known as filibusters, attempted to take matters into their own hands. One of the most infamous was William Walker, a private citizen who led a small army to Nicaragua in 1855, seized control of the government, and declared himself president.

Walker's actions, while not officially sanctioned by the U.S. government, were supported by some Southern expansionists who hoped to spread slavery into Latin America. However, his rule was short-lived, as Central American nations united to overthrow him. The Pierce administration initially recognized Walker's government but later withdrew support, demonstrating the complex and often inconsistent nature of American foreign policy in the region.

Beyond the Americas, Pierce also had to manage relations with European powers, particularly France and Britain. While he sought to maintain peaceful diplomatic relations, the growing divide between the U.S. and European nations over issues such as slavery and imperialism made foreign policy increasingly difficult.

One of the most pressing concerns was maintaining neutrality in European conflicts. The Crimean War (1853-1856) between Russia and the Ottoman Empire, Britain, and France raised questions about America's role on the global stage. While some Americans supported Russia, viewing it as a counterbalance to British and French influence, Pierce ultimately maintained a policy of neutrality, recognizing that the U.S. was not in a position to intervene in European affairs.

Conclusion

Franklin Pierce's foreign policy was a mix of ambitious expansionism and diplomatic challenges. While his administration made notable gains, such as the Gadsden Purchase and the strengthening of trade relations with Japan, it was also marked by failures like the Ostend Manifesto, which tarnished his reputation and deepened domestic divisions.

Pierce's expansionist agenda reflected the broader Democratic vision of Manifest Destiny, but it also highlighted the limits of American power and the consequences of aggressive territorial ambitions. His presidency demonstrated that while the United States was eager to assert itself on the world stage, internal conflicts—particularly the question of slavery—would continue to shape and often hinder its foreign policy decisions.

Ultimately, Pierce's foreign policy initiatives, though significant, were overshadowed by the growing sectional crisis at home. His inability to navigate both domestic and international challenges effectively contributed to his declining political standing, ensuring that his presidency would be remembered more for its failures than its successes.

Chapter 7: Political Battles and Broken Alliances

Franklin Pierce entered the presidency as a rising star within the Democratic Party, yet he left office as a man politically isolated and abandoned by many of his former allies. His tenure was marked by internal party divisions, the collapse of the Democratic stronghold, and the rapid rise of the Republican Party, which would soon redefine American politics. Though Pierce had ambitions for continued political relevance, his controversial decisions—particularly his unwavering support for pro-slavery policies—alienated both moderates and reformers, leading to his eventual fall from grace.

Conflicts Within His Own Party

Pierce's presidency began with broad Democratic support, but as the nation grew more divided over slavery, so did his own party. The issue that most fractured his administration was the Kansas-Nebraska Act of 1854.

The Democratic Party had long maintained a fragile balance between its Northern and Southern factions. Northern Democrats generally supported policies of economic expansion and limited slavery's expansion, while Southern Democrats saw slavery as essential to their economic and political power. Pierce's alignment with Southern interests created significant tension within the party, particularly as anti-slavery

Democrats in the North began to see him as a puppet of pro-slavery extremists.

The Kansas-Nebraska Act, championed by Senator Stephen A. Douglas and signed into law by Pierce, repealed the Missouri Compromise and introduced the principle of "popular sovereignty"—allowing settlers in Kansas and Nebraska to decide for themselves whether to permit slavery. Pierce believed this would defuse sectional tensions by allowing democracy to dictate the future of slavery. Instead, it had the opposite effect.

Violence erupted in Kansas as pro-slavery and anti-slavery settlers flooded into the territory to influence the vote. The bloodshed, later known as "Bleeding Kansas," exposed the deep flaws in Pierce's policy. His administration's response only worsened his political standing. Pierce openly supported the pro-slavery government in Kansas, even when it was clear that fraudulent elections and violent intimidation had been used to install it.

Many Northern Democrats felt betrayed. The once-powerful coalition of Southern and Northern Democrats was fracturing, with many moderates distancing themselves from Pierce. As his term continued, his inability to mediate between the warring factions further weakened his authority. By the end of his presidency, Pierce had lost the trust of many within his own party, making his path to reelection nearly impossible.

The Fall of the Democratic Stronghold

Pierce's support for the Kansas-Nebraska Act did not just divide his party; it fundamentally weakened the Democratic stronghold in national politics. Before his presidency, the Democratic Party had been the dominant force in American government, largely unchallenged by any strong opposition. By the end of Pierce's term, this dominance was collapsing.

The Act's passage led to widespread backlash, particularly in the North. Many former Whigs, Free Soilers, and disillusioned Democrats banded together in opposition to the expansion of slavery, forming what would soon become the Republican Party.

The midterm elections of 1854 and 1856 saw major Democratic losses, particularly in Northern states where anti-slavery sentiment was growing. Several key Democratic strongholds flipped, with many Northern Democrats defecting to the new Republican movement or joining anti-slavery coalitions. The Whig Party, which had already been in decline, effectively dissolved, leaving the political landscape open for realignment.

Pierce's support for the pro-slavery government in Kansas further eroded Democratic credibility in the North. The violence in Kansas—much of it linked to pro-slavery militias—was widely reported in the press, painting Pierce's administration as complicit in lawlessness and brutality. Even prominent Democratic figures, such as Stephen Douglas, began distancing themselves from Pierce's leadership, recognizing that his actions were costing the party support.

One of the most significant signs of the Democratic collapse was the 1856 Democratic National Convention. By this point, Pierce still hoped to secure his party's nomination for a second term. However, his unpopularity made this an uphill battle.

At the convention, Pierce was unable to rally enough support for renomination. Instead, the party chose James Buchanan, a diplomat who had been abroad during the Kansas-Nebraska controversy and was therefore less politically tainted. This was a crushing blow for Pierce—he became one of the few sitting presidents in American history to be denied his party's nomination for reelection.

The fall of the Democratic stronghold was not just about Pierce's failures; it was about the larger transformation of American politics. The old party alliances were breaking down, and sectionalism was taking center stage. The Democratic Party, once the broad and dominant coalition of American politics, was increasingly seen as the party of the South and slavery—an association that would weaken it in the coming years.

The Rise of the Republican Party and Political Isolation

The rapid rise of the Republican Party marked the final stage of Pierce's political downfall. Born out of opposition to the Kansas-Nebraska Act, the Republican Party quickly gained traction in the North, rallying anti-slavery activists, former Whigs, and disaffected Democrats.

By the time of the 1856 presidential election, the Republican Party had emerged as a formidable force, running its first national candidate, John C. Frémont. While the Democrats, led by Buchanan, ultimately won the election, the Republican Party's strong performance demonstrated that the political landscape had fundamentally changed.

Pierce, who had already been sidelined by his own party, found himself increasingly isolated as the nation moved toward even greater polarization. After leaving office, he attempted to remain politically active, but his continued support for pro-Southern policies further alienated him from the shifting mainstream.

One of the most damaging moments for Pierce came during the Civil War. Unlike other former presidents who aligned themselves with the Union cause, Pierce was highly critical of Abraham Lincoln and the Republican government. He opposed many of Lincoln's wartime measures, including the suspension of habeas corpus, and privately sympathized with the Southern cause, though he never formally endorsed secession.

His opposition to the war and his perceived Southern sympathies led to further estrangement from former allies. Many Northern Democrats who had once supported Pierce now viewed him as an embarrassment, while Republicans saw him as little more than a failed leader whose policies had helped push the country toward disunion.

Pierce's political isolation was further compounded by his personal struggles. His wife, Jane Pierce, had always been frail and deeply affected by the loss of their children, and the couple withdrew further from public life. As the war raged on, Pierce was largely forgotten in the political arena, reduced to a relic of a bygone era.

Despite his attempts to defend his legacy, Pierce's place in history was cemented as a president who had failed to navigate the growing crisis of sectionalism. His policies, particularly the Kansas-Nebraska Act, had accelerated the nation's path toward civil war. The Democratic Party, once the dominant force in American politics, had been fractured, and the Republican Party had risen to take its place in the North.

Conclusion

Franklin Pierce's political downfall was not just the result of personal missteps; it was emblematic of a broader shift in American politics. His presidency coincided with the breaking point of national unity, and his decisions—particularly his support for the Kansas-Nebraska Act—played a significant role in accelerating that division.

By the end of his tenure, Pierce had lost the confidence of his own party, been denied a second term, and found himself increasingly isolated as new political forces reshaped the nation. The rise of the Republican Party signaled a new era in American politics, one in which the old Democratic stronghold was permanently weakened.

Pierce's story is ultimately one of political miscalculation. His belief that he could hold together a divided nation by appeasing the South led to the exact opposite result—deepening divisions, weakening his party, and leaving him as one of the most politically isolated former presidents in U.S. history. His legacy remains a cautionary tale of how political ambition, when combined with an inability to adapt to the realities of a changing nation, can lead to lasting failure.

Chapter 8: A Presidency in Crisis

Franklin Pierce entered the presidency with high hopes of uniting a fractured nation. However, by the time he left office, the country was in a state of unprecedented turmoil. The crisis over slavery had escalated into outright violence, political divisions had hardened, and the Union was inching closer to a full-scale collapse. Pierce's presidency, rather than being a period of reconciliation, became a time of deepening national strife. His unwavering support for policies that favored the expansion of slavery, particularly through the Kansas-Nebraska Act, inflamed sectional tensions and directly contributed to the bloodshed that followed.

This chapter explores the defining crisis of Pierce's presidency: the violent upheaval in Kansas, his administration's struggle to maintain order, and the broader implications of his failures as the nation spiraled toward civil war.

The Bleeding Kansas Catastrophe

The passage of the Kansas-Nebraska Act in 1854 marked the beginning of one of the most violent and consequential conflicts in pre-Civil War America. By allowing the settlers of Kansas to determine whether the territory would permit slavery, the law set the stage for a bitter and bloody struggle between pro-slavery and anti-slavery forces.

Almost immediately after the act's passage, both abolitionists and pro-slavery advocates began pouring into Kansas, each seeking to sway the territory's future. Armed groups formed, and rival governments were established—one pro-slavery, based in Lecompton, and one anti-slavery, based in Topeka. The situation quickly descended into chaos, as violent clashes erupted between the two factions.

One of the most infamous episodes of this conflict was the attack on Lawrence, Kansas, in 1856. Pro-slavery forces, emboldened by the Pierce administration's tacit support, raided the town, burning buildings, destroying printing presses, and looting homes. This act of aggression was met with swift retaliation by abolitionist leader John Brown, who led his followers in the brutal Pottawatomie Massacre, where they killed five pro-slavery settlers.

The escalating violence, which came to be known as "Bleeding Kansas," shocked the nation. Newspapers from both the North and the South published horrifying accounts of the bloodshed, deepening sectional hostility. The conflict also demonstrated the complete failure of "popular sovereignty" as a solution to the slavery issue. Instead of settling the dispute through democratic means, the policy had unleashed lawlessness and destruction.

Pierce's response to the crisis only worsened his standing. Instead of acting as a neutral mediator, he sided with the pro-slavery government in Lecompton, declaring the anti-slavery movement in Kansas illegitimate. His administration ignored reports of fraud and intimidation in pro-slavery elections and dismissed calls for federal intervention to protect free-state settlers. Many in the North viewed this as proof that Pierce was a puppet of the Southern slave power.

As the violence continued, Pierce's inability to control the situation further eroded his authority. His failure to prevent bloodshed in Kansas became one of the defining failures of his presidency, cementing his legacy as a leader who had lost control over a nation on the edge of collapse.

The Struggle to Maintain Order

With Kansas descending into chaos, Pierce faced mounting pressure to take decisive action. Yet, his response was marked by inconsistency, favoritism, and an inability to effectively manage the growing crisis.

Rather than addressing the root causes of the conflict, Pierce's administration focused on legitimizing the pro-slavery government while dismissing the grievances of anti-slavery settlers. His appointment of pro-Southern officials to oversee the territory only deepened the crisis. Territorial governors were frequently replaced as they struggled to maintain control, with many of them becoming frustrated by the administration's unwillingness to acknowledge the corruption and violence plaguing Kansas.

Pierce's insistence on supporting the fraudulent pro-slavery government led to direct confrontations with Congress. Northern legislators, particularly from the newly formed Republican Party, condemned his actions as blatant favoritism toward the South. In heated congressional debates, figures like Charles Sumner denounced Pierce's policies, with Sumner famously delivering his "Crime Against Kansas" speech, in which he blamed the administration and pro-slavery forces for the bloodshed. This speech led to another shocking episode of violence when Southern Congressman Preston Brooks brutally attacked Sumner on the Senate floor, further highlighting the nation's growing divisions.

Meanwhile, Pierce's lack of effective leadership only emboldened radicals on both sides. Pro-slavery militias felt protected by the administration, while abolitionists, believing that the federal government was openly hostile to their cause, increasingly resorted to armed resistance. The political struggle had transformed into an outright battleground, with no clear path to resolution.

By the time Pierce left office in 1857, the situation in Kansas remained unresolved. His successor, James Buchanan, would inherit the crisis, but Pierce's failure to defuse the conflict had already set a dangerous precedent. The inability of the federal government to maintain peace in Kansas foreshadowed the much larger and bloodier conflict that would erupt just a few years later.

A Nation on the Brink of Civil War

The events in Kansas were not isolated—they were part of a much larger crisis gripping the United States. Pierce's presidency had exposed the deep, irreconcilable divisions between North and South, making it clear that the political system was no longer capable of containing the slavery debate.

One of the most damaging consequences of Pierce's presidency was the further breakdown of national political institutions. The Democratic Party, once a broad coalition of Northern and Southern interests, was splitting apart. Many Northern Democrats, frustrated by Pierce's handling of Kansas, defected to the new Republican Party, which was rapidly gaining momentum as the leading anti-slavery force.

At the same time, Southern leaders saw Pierce's presidency as proof that they needed to fight aggressively to protect slavery. The belief that the federal government could be used to advance Southern interests only encouraged more extreme demands from pro-slavery politicians. Many Southern leaders began openly discussing secession, convinced that the North would never accept their way of life.

The broader public also grew increasingly radicalized. Abolitionist movements gained strength in the North, fueled by outrage over events like Bleeding Kansas and the caning of Charles Sumner. Meanwhile, in the South, any attempts to limit slavery's expansion were seen as existential threats.

The debate over slavery was no longer just a political issue—it had become a battle over the future of the nation itself.

By the time of the 1856 presidential election, the political landscape had been fundamentally altered. The Democratic Party barely held onto power with the election of James Buchanan, but the rise of the Republican Party signaled the beginning of a new era. The sectional divide was no longer just a political disagreement; it was an unavoidable crisis that would soon engulf the entire country.

Pierce, now a political outcast, had little influence in shaping future events. His presidency had not just failed to prevent disunion—it had actively contributed to it. His unwavering support for pro-slavery policies had alienated Northern Democrats, strengthened the Republican movement, and emboldened Southern extremists. The nation was now heading toward an unavoidable collision, and many saw Pierce's administration as one of the key accelerants of that disaster.

Conclusion

Franklin Pierce's presidency was defined by crisis and failure. His handling of the Bleeding Kansas catastrophe demonstrated his inability to navigate the country's growing divisions, and his one-sided support for pro-slavery policies only deepened national tensions. Rather than acting as a unifier, Pierce became a polarizing figure who alienated both political allies and opponents.

His struggle to maintain order in Kansas exposed the weaknesses of his leadership, and his failure to prevent bloodshed made it clear that the nation was spiraling toward war. By the end of his presidency, the United States was more divided than ever before, with political institutions breaking down and violence becoming an accepted means of settling disputes.

While Franklin Pierce had once envisioned himself as a leader who could heal national divisions, his presidency instead accelerated the path to disunion. He left office as one of the most unpopular presidents in American history, with his legacy forever tied to the failures that pushed the nation closer to civil war.

Chapter 9: Life After the White House

Franklin Pierce left the presidency in 1857 as one of the most unpopular leaders in American history. Once hailed as a promising unifier, his tenure had only deepencd national divisions, and his legacy was one of political failure. With the rise of the Republican Party and the growing hostility between the North and South, Pierce found himself increasingly isolated, both politically and personally. The years following his presidency were marked by rejection, tragedy, and a deep sense of disillusionment.

This chapter explores Pierce's life after the White House, examining how his own party abandoned him, the personal and political consequences of his controversial stances, and the heartbreaking tragedies that defined his final years.

Rejected by His Own Party

Pierce left office expecting to maintain some influence in the Democratic Party, but he quickly found that he was no longer welcome in the political circles that once embraced him. His administration had been deeply divisive, and his unwavering support for pro-Southern policies had alienated much of the Northern faction of the party. As a result, when the Democrats gathered for their 1856 national convention, they did not even consider renominating Pierce for a second term. Instead, they turned to James Buchanan, a candidate they believed could appeal to both North and South more effectively.

Pierce, though disappointed, initially hoped to remain active in politics. However, his open opposition to the Republican Party and his continued defense of Southern interests made him an increasingly controversial figure. When the Civil War erupted in 1861, Pierce's refusal to fully support the Union cause made him an outcast in the North.

One of Pierce's most infamous moments came when he publicly criticized President Abraham Lincoln's wartime policies. He argued that Lincoln had overstepped his constitutional authority by suspending habeas corpus and expanding executive power. While some Democrats agreed with his concerns, the majority of the country saw his opposition as disloyalty at a time of national crisis.

His stance made him a pariah, even within the Democratic Party. He was no longer invited to major political events, and his former allies distanced themselves from him. In a painful irony, the man who had once been the leader of the Democratic Party now found himself abandoned by it.

The Personal and Political Fallout

The political rejection Pierce faced after his presidency was only the beginning of his troubles. His pro-Southern sympathies and vocal opposition to Lincoln's war policies earned him widespread condemnation in the North. Many viewed him as a traitor, and some accused him of secretly supporting the Confederacy. While there was no evidence that Pierce actively aided the Southern cause, his refusal to fully back the Union alienated him from both friends and former supporters.

One of the most devastating personal blows came in the form of a letter written by his longtime friend, Nathaniel Hawthorne. The renowned author had been one of Pierce's closest confidants and had even written a glowing campaign biography for him in 1852. However, as Pierce's political reputation crumbled, Hawthorne struggled to defend him. In a letter to another friend, Hawthorne admitted that while he still had affection for Pierce, he could not support his views on the war. The letter was later made public, adding to Pierce's growing sense of isolation.

Pierce's personal relationships suffered further when he attempted to reach out to former President Jefferson Davis, the leader of the Confederacy. The two men had been close during Pierce's presidency, and their friendship endured even after the war began. In 1867, after Davis was released from prison, Pierce wrote him a letter expressing sympathy for his plight. When this correspondence became public, it further cemented Pierce's reputation as a Southern sympathizer.

The political fallout was severe. Many Northern newspapers attacked him as a man who had sided with the enemies of the Union. His former allies in the Democratic Party refused to associate with him, and his once-prominent public career was effectively over.

The Tragedies of His Final Years

While the political rejection Pierce endured was painful, it was the personal tragedies of his later years that truly defined the final chapter of his life.

Even before leaving the White House, Pierce had suffered devastating losses. His three sons had all died young, with his last surviving child, Benjamin, being killed in a tragic train accident just weeks before Pierce's inauguration. The loss shattered both Pierce and his wife, Jane, who never recovered from the grief.

Jane, already a fragile and deeply religious woman, withdrew from public life entirely after their son's death. During Pierce's presidency, she rarely appeared at public events and spent much of her time in mourning. After leaving the White House, her health continued to deteriorate, and she became increasingly reclusive. In 1863, she passed away from tuberculosis, leaving Pierce completely alone.

Her death had a profound impact on him. With no children left and no wife to support him, Pierce sank into deep depression. He turned to alcohol—something that had been a struggle for him even during his presidency—to numb his pain. His drinking habits, which had long been a source of concern among his friends, worsened in his final years, and he became increasingly withdrawn from society.

Despite his isolation, a few loyal friends remained by his side. One of them was Hawthorne, who, despite their political differences, visited Pierce in 1864 while suffering from his own declining health. In a tragic turn of events, Hawthorne died during their visit, passing away in the middle of the night while staying at Pierce's home. This loss only added to Pierce's growing list of personal tragedies.

As the years went on, Pierce's health deteriorated rapidly. His years of heavy drinking took a toll on his body, and he began suffering from liver disease. By 1869, his condition had worsened significantly, and he spent his final days in seclusion at his home in Concord, New Hampshire.

On October 8, 1869, Franklin Pierce passed away at the age of 64. His death was met with little fanfare. While some newspapers acknowledged his passing, the reaction was largely muted. The nation had moved on, and Pierce, once a rising political star, had become little more than a forgotten figure in history.

Conclusion

Franklin Pierce's post-presidency was marked by rejection, personal loss, and a growing sense of irrelevance. Abandoned by his own party, condemned for his political views, and devastated by the deaths of his loved ones, he spent his final years in isolation and despair.

His legacy remains one of the most controversial in American history. While some have argued that he was a well-intentioned leader who found himself caught in an impossible situation, others see him as a failed president whose decisions accelerated the country's path to civil war.

In the end, Pierce's life after the White House serves as a tragic epilogue to a presidency that had promised unity but delivered only division. His story is a sobering reminder of how political miscalculation, personal tragedy, and historical forces beyond one's control can shape the legacy of even the most ambitious leaders.

Chapter 10: Legacy and Controversy

Franklin Pierce's presidency remains one of the most divisive in American history. Once seen as a rising political star, he left office in disgrace, his reputation tarnished by his failures to hold the Union together and his perceived Southern sympathies. His administration, marked by critical decisions such as the Kansas-Nebraska Act, is often cited as a key moment in the nation's march toward civil war. Even after his death, the debate over Pierce's leadership, political allegiances, and historical significance continues.

This chapter will examine Pierce's legacy, addressing the defining controversies of his presidency, the question of his leadership and loyalties, and the ongoing reassessment of his place in history.

A Presidency Defined by Division

Pierce's presidency was defined by division, both within the country and within his own party. Elected in 1852 as a compromise candidate meant to bridge the growing gap between North and South, he instead found himself presiding over one of the most tumultuous periods in pre-Civil War America.

One of the most significant and controversial moments of his presidency was the passage of the Kansas-Nebraska Act in 1854. The law, which repealed the Missouri Compromise and allowed new territories to determine whether they would permit slavery, led to widespread violence in Kansas and deepened sectional tensions. Pierce's enthusiastic support for the act alienated many Northern Democrats and gave rise to the Republican Party, a new political force dedicated to opposing the expansion of slavery.

The consequences of the Kansas-Nebraska Act were immediate and severe. "Bleeding Kansas" escalated into a nationwide crisis, as pro-slavery and anti-slavery groups clashed in violent confrontations. Pierce's refusal to intervene in a way that satisfied the North—combined with his administration's support for pro-slavery forces in the territory—cemented his reputation as a Southern sympathizer.

At the same time, Pierce's foreign policy efforts, such as the Ostend Manifesto, which proposed the acquisition of Cuba from Spain, further fueled suspicions that his administration was aggressively promoting Southern interests. The document, which implied that the United States might take Cuba by force if Spain refused to sell it, was widely condemned in the North as an attempt to expand slavery into the Caribbean. The backlash was so intense that the administration was forced to disavow it, but the damage to Pierce's reputation had already been done.

By the time he left office, Pierce was widely seen as a failed leader. His policies had deepened the fractures within the nation, and his party had abandoned him in favor of James Buchanan, who was viewed as a safer choice. The Democratic Party, once a dominant force in American politics, was now splintering, and Pierce bore much of the blame for its decline.

The Question of Leadership and Loyalty

Pierce's leadership has been the subject of intense scrutiny. Was he a well-intentioned leader caught in an impossible situation, or was he simply too weak and indecisive to manage the mounting crisis?

One of the biggest criticisms of Pierce is that he allowed himself to be controlled by the Southern wing of the Democratic Party. While he was a Northerner, his strong personal and political ties to Southern leaders made many question where his true loyalties lay. His cabinet was dominated by pro-slavery figures, and his administration consistently favored policies that benefited the South, even when they came at the expense of national unity.

Pierce's failure to take a strong stand against the violence in Kansas further reinforced the perception that he lacked the leadership skills necessary for the presidency. Instead of addressing the crisis head-on, he largely deferred to pro-slavery territorial leaders, allowing the situation to spiral further out of control. His reluctance to confront the issue of slavery expansion head-on only emboldened extremists on both sides.

Another key question surrounding Pierce's leadership is whether he had the political instincts necessary to navigate such a volatile era. Unlike some of his predecessors and successors, Pierce lacked a strong ideological vision for the country. He positioned himself as a moderate and sought to please all factions, but in doing so, he ultimately pleased no one. His presidency was marked by reactionary decisions rather than proactive leadership, and when faced with a national crisis, he often appeared indecisive.

The issue of loyalty also became a defining part of Pierce's post-presidential legacy. His continued friendships with prominent Confederate leaders, including Jefferson Davis, further damaged his reputation in the North. During the Civil War, he openly criticized Abraham Lincoln's wartime policies, arguing that they infringed upon civil liberties. While some of his concerns about executive overreach were valid, his criticisms were widely perceived as unpatriotic at a time when the Union was fighting for its survival.

These controversies followed him until his death, and even today, historians debate whether Pierce was simply a man of his time—struggling to hold the country together in an era of increasing polarization—or an outright failure who lacked the vision and moral conviction to lead effectively.

Reassessing His Place in History

For much of American history, Pierce has been ranked among the worst U.S. presidents. His inability to address the deepening national crisis, his support for pro-slavery policies, and his overall lack of strong leadership have placed him near the bottom of most presidential rankings. However, in recent years, some historians have taken a more nuanced view of his legacy.

One argument in Pierce's defense is that he was a product of an era in which the presidency had limited power to resolve sectional conflicts. The divisions between North and South were already deep by the time he took office, and some argue that no leader—no matter how skilled—could have prevented the Civil War from occurring in the coming years.

Others have pointed out that Pierce, unlike some of his contemporaries, did not personally own slaves and did not aggressively advocate for slavery's expansion in the way that figures like John C. Calhoun or Jefferson Davis did. Instead, he saw himself as a constitutionalist who was trying to uphold the existing legal framework, even if that meant making concessions to the South.

Still, these arguments do little to change the fact that Pierce's actions helped accelerate the collapse of the Union. His policies emboldened pro-slavery extremists, weakened the Democratic Party, and helped set the stage for the rise of Abraham Lincoln and the Republican Party.

In modern historical assessments, Pierce is often viewed as a cautionary tale—a leader who prioritized party unity and political alliances over the moral and practical realities of a divided nation. His failures illustrate the dangers of appeasement in the face of growing extremism and the consequences of choosing compromise at all costs.

Even as historians continue to reassess his presidency, one thing remains clear: Franklin Pierce's legacy is one of controversy, division, and lost potential. He entered the White House as a popular and promising figure, but by the time he left, he was widely regarded as a disappointment. His name is rarely mentioned among the great American presidents, and his legacy serves as a reminder of how political miscalculation and lack of decisive leadership can shape history in profound ways.

Conclusion

Franklin Pierce's legacy is one of contradictions. He was a Northern politician who aligned with the South, a president who sought unity but deepened division, and a man whose leadership has been questioned for more than a century. His presidency, marked by critical missteps such as the Kansas-Nebraska Act and the Ostend Manifesto, played a significant role in the nation's path to civil war.

While some modern historians have offered a more sympathetic view of Pierce, acknowledging the difficult political landscape he faced, the general consensus remains that he failed to rise to the occasion. His inability to provide strong leadership in a time of crisis sealed his fate as one of the most ineffective presidents in U.S. history.

Ultimately, Pierce's story is not just a personal tragedy but a national one. His presidency serves as a lesson in the dangers of weak leadership, misplaced loyalties, and the high cost of political compromise in a deeply divided country.

Made in the USA
Columbia, SC
22 June 2025